Fact Finders®

Kids' Guide to Government

UNDERSTANDING YOUR LEGAL RIGHTS

By John Micklos Jr.

CAPSTONE PRESS
a capstone imprint

Fact Finders Books are published by Capstone Press,
1710 Roe Crest Drive, North Mankato, Minnesota 56003
www.mycapstone.com

Library of Congress Cataloging-in-Publication Data
Names: Micklos, John, author.
Title: Understanding your legal rights / by John Micklos, Jr.
Description: North Mankato, Minnesota : Capstone Press, [2018] |
Series: Kids' guide to government
Identifiers: LCCN 2017046960 (print) | LCCN 2017047982 (ebook) |
ISBN 9781543503258 (eBook PDF) | ISBN 9781543503333 (reflowable Epub) |
ISBN 9781543503173 (library binding) | ISBN 9781543503210 (paperback)
Subjects: LCSH: Law—United States—Juvenile literature. | Civil law—United States—
Juvenile literature. | Civil rights—United States—Juvenile literature.
Classification: LCC KF387 (ebook) | LCC KF387 .M53 2018 (print) |
DDC 342.7308/5—dc23
LC record available at https://lccn.loc.gov/2017046960)

Editorial Credits
Michelle Hasselius, editor; Mackenzie Lopez, designer;
Jo Miller, media researcher; Kathy McColley, production specialist

Photo Credits
Getty Images: DEA PICTURE LIBRARY/Contributor, 6-7, Michael Zagaris/
Contributor, 9, Tim Boyle/Staff, 21; Library of Congress Prints and Photographs,
5; Shutterstock: a katz, 19, Africa Studio, 20, Andrey_Popov, 18, ByEmo, 23, Celig,
cover, Cynthia Farmer, 13, Egyptian Studio, 12, Everett Historical, 15, Macrovector, 24,
Photographee.eu, 25, Popartic, 16, Selta, 10-11

Design Elements
Capstone

Printed and bound in Canada.
010801S18

TABLE OF CONTENTS

Chapter 1

Founded on Freedom

Everybody in the United States has legal rights —
even children. We receive our legal rights from the U.S.
Constitution and laws passed by the federal and state
government.

We haven't always had the rights we have today. In the
mid-1700s, Great Britain ruled America's 13 **colonies**.
The British made the laws.

The colonists had to pay increasingly high taxes to Great Britain but had no voice in the British government. The colonists protested and demanded the same rights as British **citizens**. They grew angrier. This eventually led to the Revolutionary War and America's fight for its independence.

an engraving of the Battle of Lexington

The Revolutionary War

In April 1775 fighting broke out between British troops and American colonists in Lexington and Concord, Massachusetts. This marked the first shots of the Revolutionary War. The war between the colonists and Great Britain raged for years. In 1783 Great Britain agreed to recognize America as an independent nation. The two sides signed the Treaty of Paris, ending the war.

colony—an area that has been settled by people from another country; a colony is ruled by another country
citizen—a member of a country or state who is protected by it and has obligations to it

The Revolutionary War was over. The United States had gained its freedom from Great Britain. But how should the new nation be governed? In 1787 **delegates** from the 13 colonies drafted the U.S. Constitution. The document established the nation's government and created laws that guaranteed basic rights to its citizens.

On September 17, 1787, 38 delegates signed the U.S. Constitution.

The first 10 **amendments** to the U.S. Constitution are called the Bill of Rights. The Bill of Rights spells out the basic rights all Americans have. These amendments were **ratified** and became part of the Constitution in 1791. Over time other amendments have been added. There are now 27 amendments to the Constitution. Let's learn about some of the legal rights given to us from the U.S. Constitution, as well as the federal government.

delegate—a person who represents other people at a meeting
amendment—a formal change made to a law or a legal document
ratify—formally approve

Chapter 2

The First Amendment

The First Amendment gives people several rights under the Constitution, including freedom of speech, the right to **assemble,** freedom of religion, and freedom of the press. In the United States, people can question or even criticize the government and its leaders.

Free speech allows people to express themselves through words or actions, but it does have limits. It is illegal to use speech to cause violence. Free speech must not place others in danger. For example, you can't legally yell "fire" in a crowded building if there isn't a fire. People could panic and get hurt.

Children and Free Speech

You have limited rights to free speech. You still have to follow the rules set by your parents and teachers. For example, you may want to write something in your school newspaper. But the teacher in charge of the paper gets to decide what is published.

Eli Harold (left), Colin Kaepernick (center), and Eric Reid (right) kneeled during the National Anthem before a football game on September 25, 2016.

Taking a Stand by Not Standing

The National Anthem is often played at the beginning of sporting events. Players as well as **spectators** stand and place their hands over their hearts. In 2016 San Francisco 49ers quarterback Colin Kaepernick chose not to stand when the anthem was played. He said he was protesting the unfair treatment of African-Americans in the U.S. Although his actions upset some people, his right to protest was protected against government penalties.

assemble—to come together
spectator—a person who watches an event

The Right to Peacefully Assemble

On January 21, 2017, people of all races and ages took part in the Women's March, which supported women's rights. Some carried signs. Others chanted as they walked. They marched in Washington, D.C., and many other cities around the U.S. and worldwide. Thousands of kids also took part. The Women's March drew nearly 5 million protesters throughout the nation and around the world.

FACT

In 2003 as many as 10 to 15 million people marched in cities across the world to protest the war in Iraq.

According to the Constitution, people are allowed to gather and march publicly to support or protest issues. Marches show the power of people working together for a cause. The voices of thousands — or millions — of people carry a lot of weight. These marches and protests are legal as long as they remain peaceful.

Sometimes kids march with their parents. In the 1960s many children took part in **civil rights** marches. These marches supported equal rights for African-Americans in the U.S. A few years later, some children took part in marches to end the Vietnam War.

civil rights—the rights that all Americans have to freedom and equal treatment under the law

11

Freedom of Religion

The First Amendment gives people the freedom to believe in any religion they wish. The government cannot tell us what we should or should not believe. The Constitution created a separation of church and state. This means the U.S. government cannot require or favor any one religion. Today public schools and government offices often avoid celebrating religious events so no one feels excluded.

Religion and Schools

Schools and school events can't sponsor prayers. However, religious student clubs may meet before and after school to pray. Because they are not run by the government, private and religious schools do not have the same rules about religion. They can celebrate religious practices however they wish.

Chapter 3
Your Rights at Home, School, and Work

Some days you may not feel like going to school. But going to school was not always an option for kids. Until the early 1900s, many children in the United States did not go to school. Often kids younger than 10 years old had to work full time. Child workers earned low wages. Some had to work in factories, fields, or mines. Many suffered serious injuries and some were killed because of dangerous working conditions.

In 1938 Congress passed the Fair Labor Standards Act. The act included a set of child labor laws. These laws limited the number of hours that children could work. It outlawed working conditions that were dangerous to children.

Today kids can't work in most jobs until they are 16 years old. From age 16 to the day they turn 18, they may work only limited hours.

Many children worked in cotton mills in the early 1900s.

The Fair Labor Standards Act also set a **minimum wage** that employees must receive for their work. Employees may make more than this amount, but they cannot make less. People have other rights in the workplace. These rights do not depend on gender or age. For example, workers have a right to safe working conditions.

In many jobs, men earn more money than women.

The Gender Pay Gap

Imagine a woman sitting at her desk at work. A man sitting next to her is doing the same job. Do they make the same amount of money? Not always. In 2016 it was estimated that a woman in the U.S. earns 80.5 cents to every dollar that a man earns for doing the same job.

Kid-Sized Jobs

If you're under 16 years old, there are still ways you can earn money. Before starting any job, make sure to get a parent's permission.

- ★ Look into babysitting your younger siblings or neighbors.
- ★ Talk to your parents about washing cars for others in the neighborhood.
- ★ Offer to mow grass or do gardening work.
- ★ When the snow starts to fall, offer to shovel driveways.

minimum wage—the lowest amount a company can legally pay a worker

Search and Seizure

The Fourth Amendment in the Constitution protects people from illegal searches and **seizures**. This means police officers cannot search you or your property without a reason. In most cases police need a **search warrant** to enter your home. A search warrant is a legal paper signed by a judge allowing the police to enter. To get this warrant, the police need to show **probable cause**.

There are situations when police can enter a home without a search warrant. Police do not need a warrant if they have the owner's permission to enter the home, if there is an emergency, or if the police see illegal activity.

Police investigators searched for a suspect in New York in 2013.

seizure—the act of taking something away from someone
search warrant—an official document issued by a judge that allows the police to search property where they expect to find evidence of a crime
probable cause—showing that a search is likely to yield evidence of a crime

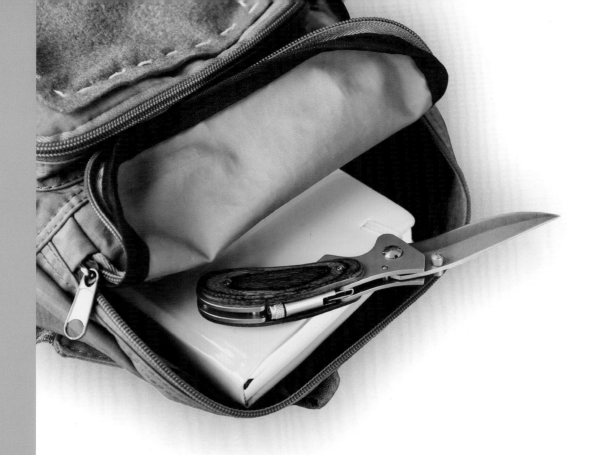

Searches at School

Imagine that two students tell a teacher that another student brought a knife to school. The teacher notifies the principal, who searches the student's backpack and locker. Is this a legal search? The answer is yes. Courts have ruled that school officials may search student backpacks and lockers if there is reason to do so.

Students walked through metal detectors in their Chicago high school in 2002.

Deadly Violence at School

In 2012 Adam Lanza entered Sandy Hook Elementary School in Connecticut. Using a rifle, Lanza killed 20 young students and six staff members.

School shootings have led to concerns about students' safety at school. Schools across the country conduct drills to teach students and teachers what to do if dangerous intruders enter their schools. Most schools have rules restricting anyone but students and staff from accessing the buildings without permission. Some schools even have metal detectors to identify weapons.

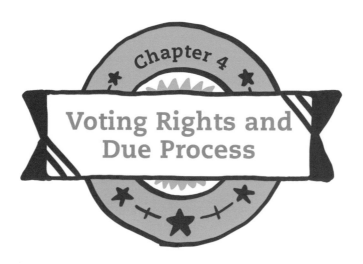

Voting Rights and Due Process

Voting: A Right and a Responsibility

People in the United States get to choose who represents them in the government at the local, state, and federal levels. This is done by voting. Voting is a right, but there are restrictions. You must be at least 18 years old and a U.S. citizen to vote in government elections.

democracy—a form of government in which citizens can choose their leaders by voting

If you are not old enough to vote yet, you can still be part of the **democratic** process. Talk to your teacher about upcoming school elections. Make your voice heard by casting your vote for class president, vice president, and other positions. If you are interested in politics, you can even run for one of these positions at school.

Every Vote Matters!

In the 2016 presidential election, more than 130 million Americans voted for president. That may seem like a lot, but that is only 55 percent of all eligible voters. That means that almost half of the people who could vote didn't.

FACT

Many elections have been close races. Some winners have been decided by a few votes. In 1839 Marcus "Landslide" Morton won the election for governor of Massachusetts by a single vote!

Both the Fifth Amendment and 14th Amendment guarantee due process of law. That provides certain rights to people who are accused of crimes. For example, it prevents the government from taking someone's freedom or property without going through the legal process. A **suspect** must also be told why he or she is being arrested. The suspect has the right to a trial by jury and can speak in his or her own defense.

People who are found innocent of a crime cannot be tried again for the same crime. For example, a person may not be tried twice for the same robbery. He or she could, however, be tried for a different robbery.

a jury trial taking place in a courtroom

People who are found guilty of crimes also have rights. Criminals cannot receive cruel punishments and must be given food, water, and basic medical care. Depending on the crime, youth who are found by the court to have committed a crime may be sent to a **juvenile detention center**. This keeps them with people their own age rather than with adults.

a police officer talks to a woman at a police station

suspect—someone accused of a crime
juvenile detention center—a place where people under age 18 who have committed crimes are kept as punishment

Chapter 5

Know Your Rights

It's important to know your legal rights. It's the only way to know you are receiving fair treatment. To learn more about your rights, go to the library. You could also ask your parents to take you to a police station or courthouse to see our legal rights in action.

If you think one of your legal rights has been **violated**, talk to your parents or teachers. They can help you decide if a law has been broken and what you might do about it.

violate—to be harmed by someone

The Bill of Rights

The amendments in the Bill of Rights can be hard to understand. Here is what they are and what they mean.

First Amendment

"Congress shall make no law respecting an establishment of religion, or prohibiting the free exercise thereof; or abridging the freedom of speech, or of the press; or the right of the people peaceably to assemble . . ."

What it means: The government cannot tell people what they should or should not believe. This amendment also gives people the right to gather together and speak freely. It guarantees media freedom.

Second Amendment

". . . the right of the people to keep and bear arms, shall not be infringed."

What it means: This amendment protects a citizen's right to have firearms.

Third Amendment

"No solider shall, in time of peace be quartered in any house, without the consent of the owner . . ."

What it means: The U.S. government cannot place troops into private homes without the owner's permission.

Fourth Amendment

"The right of the people to be secure in their persons, houses, papers, and effects, against unreasonable searches and seizures, shall not be violated, and no Warrants shall issue, but upon probable cause . . ."

What it means: Officials may not search a person's possessions unless the search is reasonable. In home searches, a warrant based on probable cause is usually required.

Fifth Amendment

". . . No person shall be . . . subject for the same offence to be twice put in jeopardy of life or limb; nor shall be compelled in any criminal case to be a witness against himself, nor be deprived of life, liberty, or property, without due process of law . . ."

What it means: People who are accused of crimes must be given due process. They can choose not to testify against themselves in court. They cannot be tried twice for the same crime.

Sixth Amendment

In all criminal prosecutions, the accused shall enjoy the right to a speedy and public trial, by an impartial jury of the State and district wherein the crime shall have been committed, which district shall have been previously ascertained by law, and to be informed of the nature and cause of the accusation; to be confronted with the witnesses against him; to have compulsory process for obtaining witnesses in his favor, and to have the Assistance of Counsel for his defence.

What it means: People have the right to a speedy, fair, and open trial. They also have the right to have a lawyer defend them.

Seventh Amendment

"In Suits at common law, where the value in controversy shall exceed twenty dollars, the right of trial by jury shall be preserved, and no fact tried by a jury, shall be otherwise re-examined in any Court of the United States, than according to the rules of the common law."

What it means: Civil cases may be tried in front of a jury, just like criminal trials.

Eighth Amendment

"Excessive bail shall not be required, nor excessive fines imposed, nor cruel and unusual punishments inflicted."

What it means: Courts must set reasonable amounts for bail and fines. Punishments for crimes must be fair and humane.

Ninth Amendment

"The enumeration in the Constitution, of certain rights, shall not be construed to deny or disparage others retained by the people."

What it means: People have rights beyond the ones listed in the U.S. Constitution.

Tenth Amendment

"The powers not delegated to the United States by the Constitution, nor prohibited by it to the States, are reserved to the States respectively, or to the people."

What it means: The federal government has only the powers listed in the U.S. Constitution. Those powers not specifically granted to the federal government belong to the states, or to the people.

Glossary

amendment (uh-MEND-muhnt)—a formal change to a law or legal document

assemble (uh-SEM-buhl)—to come together

citizen (SI-tuh-zuhn)—a member of a country or state who is protected by it and has obligations to it

civil rights (SIV-il-RYTS)—the rights that all Americans have to freedom and equal treatment under the law

colony (KAH-luh-nee)—an area that has been settled by people from another country; a colony is ruled by another country

delegate (DEL-uh-gate)—someone who represents other people at a meeting

democracy (di-MOK-ruh-see)—a form of government in which citizens can choose their leaders by voting

juvenile detention center (JOO-vuh-nuhl di-TEN-shuhn SEN-tur)—a place where people under age 18 who committed crimes are kept as punishment

minimum wage (MIN-uh-muhm WAJE)—the lowest amount a company can legally pay a worker

probable cause (PROB-uh-buhl KAWZ)—showing that a search is likely to yield evidence of a crime

ratify (RAT-uh-fye)—formally approve

search warrant (SURCH WOR-uhnt)—an official document issued by a judge that allows the police to search property where they expect to find evidence of a crime

seizure (SEE-zhur)—the act of taking something away from someone

spectator (SPEK-tay-tur)—a person who watches an event

suspect (SUHSS-pekt)—someone accused of a crime

violate (VYE-uh-late)—to be harmed by someone

Critical Thinking Questions

1. You have the right to vote in the U.S., but there are restrictions. Who can vote in government elections?

2. To get a search warrant, police officers must show probable cause. What does "probable cause" mean?

3. Describe two rights that due process provides to people who are accused of crimes.

Read More

Baxter, Roberta. *The Bill of Rights.* Documenting U.S. History. Chicago: Heinemann Library, 2013.

Krull, Kathleen. *A Kids' Guide to America's Bill of Rights.* New York: Harper, 2015.

Leavitt, Amie Jane. *The Bill of Rights in Translation: What It Really Means.* Kids' Translations. North Mankato, Minn.: Capstone Press, 2018.

Internet Sites

Use FactHound to find Internet sites related to this book.

Visit *www.facthound.com.*

Just type in 9781543503173 and go.

Check out projects, games and lots more at
www.capstonekids.com

31

Index